THE
LOST BROTHERS
OF THE
ALLEGHANIES

FROM REAL LIFE
SAD BUT TRUE

By JAMES A. SELL
Hollidaysburg, Pa.
R. D. No. 1

Memorial Services held May 8, 1906, being
the Fiftieth Anniversary of the Finding

BRETHREN PUBLISHING HOUSE
ELGIN, ILLINOIS

THE MEMORIAL MONUMENT.

The Inscription:

On the south side: "The lost children of the Alleghanies were found here May 8, 1856."

On the east side: "Joseph S. Cox, aged 5 yrs. 6 mo. and 9 da.; George C. Cox, aged 7 yrs. 1 mo. and 19 da.; children of Samuel and Susan Cox."

On the north side: "Wandered from home April 24, 1856."

On the west side: "Dedicated May 8, 1906."

THE LOST BROTHERS OF THE ALLEGHANIES

WESTERN Pennsylvania is a very mountainous country. The Appalachian system crosses it from south to north. The Alleghany range is a part of this system, and is from fifty to eighty miles wide. It is very irregular in its construction, consisting of knobs and ravines of various heights and depths in almost endless variety.

Between the peaks there are fine slopes and fertile valleys of larger or smaller proportions. In its primitive state the mountain was densely covered with timber. In places, even on the elevations, there were swamps which were overgrown with briars and laurel, forming a deep tangle of underbrush. This was the favorite retreat for the wild animals when chased by the hunter. It was not safe for persons unacquainted to venture alone far into this wilderness. They would lose their bearing, become bewildered and have difficulty to find their way out.

The pioneer settlers were mostly hunters and lumbermen who blazed their way into the unexplored forests, erected small cabins by piling up logs, notched together at the corners and covered with clapboards,—boards split from trees. People who were brought up in such homes usually staid by them, or pushed farther on and opened up a new place with some improvement; and thus one generation succeeded another until some places became fairly well settled, and small towns sprang up. But much of the mountain proper yet remains in its virgin state.

Samuel Cox and wife were natives of Bedford County, Pa. They were mountaineers by birthright. Hearing of the broad plains free from rocks that awaited settlers in the West, they concluded to quit the hills of their native State and go to a more inviting field. With their four children they located, in 1855, somewhere in the State of Indiana. Here sickness overtook them, and, in the interests of their children's health, they were advised to return to their old home. In the autumn of the same year they returned and pushed into the wilderness and took up their temporary abode in an old vacated cabin, in view of making a purchase of a tract of land surrounding it. Here they lived lonely but happily through the winter. On the morning of April 24, while they were at breakfast, the dog treed some game in the surrounding woods, and Mr. Cox started in pursuit with his trusty rifle. His two little boys, Joseph and George, aged respectively five and seven years, unknown to him followed.

The mother, thinking they were with their father, gave herself no concern, until he returned. And here begins a tragedy that moved more hearts to sympathy and moistened more eyes with tears and stamped itself more indelibly on the minds of the people of this community than any other thing that ever occurred in central Pennsylvania. The terrible Johnstown flood, that was not many miles away, where millions of dollars' worth of property and thousands of lives were lost in thirty minutes' time, was not even a parallel.

The parents meeting with no success, gave the alarm and neighbors turned to assist, and the search was continued day and night with constantly increasing numbers for fourteen days.

By this time the crowd had swelled to about five thousand people. They were divided into companies of fifty each, and given under charge of some man well acquainted with the mountains. They spread out and worked in the most systematic manner possible. They searched by day and kept campfires burning at night. No clue was found, and where the children could be

SAMUEL COX
Father of the Lost Children

was a mystery so dark and deep that it baffled the wisdom of all.

The interest was becoming intense. Three counties were thoroughly aroused and from more distant points volunteers were pouring in. The altitude of the mountain causes it to be much cooler than it is in the valleys just east. More snow falls in the winter and continues longer in the spring. It was cool and damp all the time the little boys were gone, and several nights were freezing cold.

Bobs Creek rises north of this and flows in a southerly direction. It is the head waters of the Raystown branch of the Juniata River. The spring rains and melting snows increased the volume of water, making it a wild dashing stream about 30 feet wide. There were no bridges in the vicinity. The Cox family lived several miles on the west side of the stream. It was the united opinion of all who saw it that the children could not have crossed it, and they confined their search to the west side. In fear that they might have fallen into the stream, it was thoroughly searched.

Impossible as it seemed to be for the children to cross the stream, the decision was to begin on the morning of the fourteenth day to search on the eastern side. Before this was begun another episode broke in

SUSAN COX
Mother of the Lost Children

that adds another chapter to the already strange and mysterious occurrence. Mr. Dibert, who lived some miles east of the mountain, was kept from assisting in the search through sickness. One night he had a remarkable dream about the lost ones. He told no one about it. It was repeated the third time. Feeling that it was a revelation to him, he told his brother-in-law, Mr. Wysong, who was familiar with the place. The two started out in what was to Mr. Dibert a strange country, to follow the trail of his dream. In ran in this way: By passing a certain contour of the mountain they would find a dead deer, then a little shoe, then a small beech tree that had fallen across Bobs Creek, over which the children had passed. So they went from one object to another, which were all found as they appeared in the dream. Farther on an old birch tree, close by a hemlock in a deep ravine by a little stream of water, is standing, and there the dream ended with the lost ones found. And, true enough, when the spot was reached, here the little brothers lay. The small beech tree that spanned the stream had been seen in the search, but being so small where it touched the opposite shore. and lying eight or ten feet above the water, where the stream was about thirty-five feet wide, it was deemed to be an impossible crossing place.

A little patch torn from one of their garments was

found on a snag of the tree, and was a circumstance
that confirmed beyond a doubt, that this was their
crossing place. It will be observed that the searching
was all done on the wrong side of the stream.

For fourteen days all work was stopped. The plows
stood still in the furrows; the builders laid down their
tools; the miner came out of the mines; the woodsman
laid aside his saw and axe; the merchant closed his
store, and all entered the forest as volunteer searchers.
Mothers and sisters out of sympathy for the heartbroken mother, and pity for the suffering boys, baked
and sent out bread and delicacies for the men who
braved the elements to search for the lost. Thus men
and women, young men and maidens, mingled in the
work, in sympathy, in prayers and in tears over the
cruel fate that cast a shadow deeper and more mysterious than ever came over this fair land and finds its
equal hardly once in a century.

It will never be known how long the children wandered around before they died. They were about ~~five~~
ten miles from home. From appearances, the younger died
first. His head was pillowed on a stone and his
brother lay a little more indifferent with one hand in
the water.

Few mothers indeed have the experience of this one.
Kind friends did what they could to comfort her, but

soon found that there could be no comfort. She persistently cried for her little boys and never closed an eye in sleep while they were gone.

It is a sad, yet sweet service, for a mother to minister to the wants of her dying child. But here are two little boys alone in a wilderness, suffering—who knows what?—loneliness, fear, cold and hunger, with a loving, heartbroken, grief-stricken mother only a few miles away. Their piteous cries unheard, with no loving touch to soothe the pangs of death. Let us hope some kind angel ministered to them and that their little lives went out in sweetness.

> " It must be sweet in childhood, to give back
>   The spirit to its Maker; ere the heart
>   Has grown familiar with the paths of sin,
>   And sown to garner up its bitter fruits."

An old king once sat with a company of invited guests in his hall, dimly lighted and open at both ends. A bird flew in and out again. An old man present compared the bird's flight to our passage through the world. We come out of darkness into the dim light of this life, and when the brief journey is completed, we go into the darkness of the unknown future. So with these little boys; they came into this great hall of life and staid long enough to know the sweetness of a mother's love. And this was all they did know. They

JACOB DIBERT
Through whose dreams the
Lost Children were found

HARRISON WYSONG
Who acted as guide for
Mr. Dibert

knew not whence they came, or whither they were going, or why the journey must be made, or why it must
end so soon and so sadly, attended with so much suffering.   Their only prayers were their piteous cries
as they lifted up their innocent, helpless hands, and
marked their footsteps with their bleeding feet.

This is the history of every life.   The only differ-
ence is in the point of time.   It takes some a little
longer to make the journey.   But every life, no matter
how rich in love, or sparkling with joy, will at last
come to its close and become a tragedy attended with a
deep and sad mystery that weeping friends on the
earthly side can never solve.

Here is our only comfort:

> " In hope of heaven I find relief,
>   Although my heart is bound with grief,
>   A balm for every wound is sent
>   With Christ my Shepherd I'm content.
>
> " I'll hold the hand that leadeth me
>   O'er life's eventful, troubled sea;
>   And pray for strength to live aright,
>   Tho' curtains dark obscure the light."

When the boys were found signals were given by
tolling bells and tooting horns, and responded to by
thousands of human voices.   The untiring searchers
turned in hot haste to the place.   The news was joyful,

but every heart was sad that life had gone. The little bodies were wrapped in blankets, placed on a sled, and the homeward journey was begun. While they were passing over the rocky roads through the dense wilderness to the earthly home, the uncaged and dove-like spirits were away on the cloudy fields of ether. joining in the songs which angels know. They are happy and free from the snares of earth. But, oh, think of the mother, who, after spending so many sleepless nights sitting in the loneliness of her forest home, waiting in this awful suspense, receiving to her arms the lifeless forms of her darling boys, who through innocence. dependence and affection, had brought so much sunshine into her life.

Time moved slowly and heavily. At length the train bearing its precious trust drew up to the cabin door. Here, gentle reader, we will let the curtain drop. What is behind is too sad and sacred to be expressed in words.

> " Take them, O death, and bear away
> Whate'er thou canst call thine own,
> Thine image stamped upon this clay
> Doth give thee that, but that alone.

> "Take them, O grave, and let them lie,
> Folded upon thy narrow shelves,
> As garments by the soul laid by,
> And precious only to themselves.

" Take them, O great eternity,
      Our little life is but a gust,
      That bends the branches of thy tree,
      And trails its blossoms in the dust."

The forest where the children wandered and were found, remained in this primeval state until recently. The heavy timber is being converted into lumber, and a railroad has penetrated the very ravine where the children were found. It was suggested by someone that there should be a reserve of the land and trees where this remarkable occurrence took place. The owner very generously donated the ground and very soon the project of erecting a monument with appropriate inscriptions was started and soon consummated. The cost was one hundred and twenty dollars. Contributions flowed in, and it would have been an easy matter, especially since the dedication, to raise money for one more costly.

May 8, 1906, was the fiftieth anniversary of the finding, and of the fulfillment of a remarkable dream. The monument was erected, and the day was set apart for the memorial services. There was a great gathering of people. Men, women and children by the thousands, some from quite a distance, came to this sacred spot. All were anxious to see the monument and the tree under which the children lay, and to touch the stone the younger had for his dying pillow. Sadness filled every heart, and many were moved to tears. All seemed to catch the inspiration, and here the angel of death took two little innocent sufferers to the sweet home of the blessed Jesus, who said, " Of such is the kingdom of heaven."

The erecting of monuments is a common thing but they are mostly dedicated to great events, or to men of renown, or where battles are fought, or leaders of armies have fallen. This, however, is an exception. The world can hardly show a parallel. They were little innocent children. They were unknown to the world. They came from a humble home,—very much so indeed. A more secluded and out-of-the-way place would be hard to find. Their death moved the hearts of thousands of people in their day, and the memory of them lives and moves the hearts of people fifty years after, to go to the expense of this monument to tell to generations following what occurred at this sacred spot.

Ours is a sinful world, —a wicked, unfeeling world; but there are times when we rise above the dust and smoke of the world's passion and strife and see humanity in its better light. There is, let us trust, a better day for our fallen race. If two little boys going to wander for a few days in the mountains, and then to lie down by a little brook to die, have the power to

move and hold a people for fifty years and touch a
generation not then born that they will come many
miles with evidences of tender hearts, . surely this
points to the coming of a brighter day.

> " Hope is singing, ever singing;
>   Singing in an undertone,
>   Singing as if God had taught it,
> ' It is better farther on.' "

Fifty years have come and gone, and some of us
who were children then are beginning to feel the
weight of time. Those who helped to search for the
lost ones have mostly passed over the mystic river and
through the dark valley that separates this world from
the next. Those who are left are stooped with age and
are leaning heavily on their canes and wearing silver
locks about their heads. The lady who conveyed the
news of the finding to the mother is still living, but
has exchanged the blushing charms of maidenhood
for the furrows that fifty years scored on her counte-
nance. She has about covered the span allotted to man-
kind, and is waiting, in faith and hope for the call to
join the dear ones who have gone before and to enjoy
the happy recognition that awaits them beyond the vale
and mist that hangs about the earthly side.

For fifty years the winds have swept up the forest
aisles and played among the branches of the trees

sweet music as a requiem over the place. The snows of fifty winters have robed them in purity,—beautiful emblem of the pure souls that have left the earth for the home of the pure above. The little brook on the bank of which the children lay still gurgles its liquid song and makes music sweet and sad. It reminds one of the stream that issues from the eternal throne along which, for fifty years as we measure time, the lost children have been basking under fairer skies and roaming over lovelier landscapes in the enduring home from which they shall never wander to suffer fear, cold and starvation.

These lofty heights have witnessed the sunsets of fifty years as the sun has flashed down his light and painted a halo of glory around these cliffs and hung great pictures on the walls of the sky. It makes one feel after all that our kind Father, who knows what is best, brought the children out here to meet the angel reaper, to impress the thousands who visit the place that there is a land over which his glory sheds a light that is more glorious and beautiful than the fiery dawns and golden sunsets among the mountains of a sin-cursed world. It may be found after all that the terrible ordeal will be worth more than it cost.

> " His purposes will ripen fast,
>   Unfolding every hour;

The bud may have a bitter taste,
But sweet will be the flower."

For fifty years the trees have put forth their leaves, which again turned to crimson and yellow and went back to dust, emblematical of us all. The tree under which the lives of the little sufferers went out is an evergreen. Beautiful emblem, too, of the soul that never dies and of the home of ever-blooming flowers and unfading verdure.

" And all whose hopes are centered there
Shall rise o'er grief and pain,
For in that land no earthly care
Shall vex our souls again."

The day of dedication was lovely. Nature was at her best. The sun shone brightly from a clear sky. The air was pure, crisp and bracing. Systematic arrangements were made for the ceremonies. The crowd was large, but very orderly; there was no jar or discord in any movement. The solemnity of a funeral pervaded every breast. The signal for the opening service was given by the band of musicians. When the stillness of this vast wilderness was broken by the dolorous sound of the piping horns and the muffled drum, a solemn stillness fell upon the vast assembly, and tears fell like autumn rain. The surrounding heights that often took up the sound of the hunter's gun and the woodman's axe, and echoed it through their fastness, at once entered into the spirit of the occasion, and bore through all their corridors the sweet cadences of the music and rolled them back to the rapt assembly. We were made to think,—and there was joy in the thought,—of the music of heaven when the redeemed shall break loose on the new song and the sweet strains like the voice of many waters shall roll upward in the volume of a great thunder, and attended with the harpers, heaven's dome will be filled and the echo will fill the soul with an ecstacy that will last through eternity.

During life the little brothers were noticeably affectionate with each other. They always walked with joined hands. They clung to each other in their wanderings in the awful solitudes of a wilderness. Together they braved the crossing of a dashing mountain stream, where people of judgment would not have ventured. They staid by each other when the pangs of cold and hunger caused them to lie down to the sleep that had no waking. Truly "they were loving in their lives and in their deaths they were not divided." They were placed in one coffin and in the presence of three thousand people were affectionately given to the grave. How they escaped the hungry appetites of the wild beasts of the forest must have been

purely providential. The parents are now dead and
are laid at rest beside the dear ones who were taken
from them under circumstances of indescribable sadness.

> " The storm that wrecks the wintry sky
>   No more disturbs their sweet repose,
> Than summer evening's latest sigh.
>   That shuts the rose."

The writer of this imperfect sketch lives sixteen
miles from the place where the boys were found and
where the monument is erected. He well remembers
the exciting time from April 24, 1856, to May 8, of the
same year, but he was then too young to join the
searchers. And, now, after a lapse of fifty years, to
visit the place with congenial friends and especially
those who have assisted in the search and were present
when the little ones were found, forms an association
around which cling our sweetest joys, our tenderest
emotions and our purest faith.

The experiences of the day produced mingled feel-
ings of joy and sadness. We mingled our sympathies,
our prayers and our tears. Our faith in humanity is
made stronger. We parted. Many of us will never
meet again in this world. There were present people
of wealth and culture and many from the humbler
walks of life. There were the aged, whose bent forms
and wrinkled faces were quite in contrast with the

young, whose cheeks were blushing with the vermilion
of blooming life. But the grim reaper with his scythe
is after us all, and his stroke is irrevocable

> " The boast of heraldry, the pomp of pcwer,
>   And all that beauty, all that wealth e'er gave,
>   Await alike the inevitable hour,
>   The paths of glory lead but to the grave."

One man amidst the interest and solemnity of the
dedicatory services yielded to his appetite for drink
and lay by the wayside in a drunken sleep. A lady
remarked that he was lost in a worse sense than were
the little children. True, and true of us all. " All we
like sheep have gone astray." And if we are not found
by the blessed Christ we are lost to the pleasure of his
service here and his presence in the home beyond. He
came to seek and save that which was lost.

> " But none of the ransomed ever knew
>   How deep were the waters crossed,
>   Or how dark was the night which the Lord
>   passed through,
>   Ere he found his sheep that was lost
>   Out in the desert he heard its cry,
>   Sick and helpless and ready to die.

> " And all through the mountains thunder-riven
>   And up from the rocky steep,
>   There arose a cry to the gate of heaven,
>   ' Rejoice, I have found my sheep.'
>   And the angels echoed around the throne,
>   ' Rejoice, for the Lord brings back his own.' "

Hollidaysburg, Pa.

OUR BEAUTIFUL HOME

❦ ❦ ❦

" Beyond the dark river of death—
  Beyond where its waters are swelling,
  The home of my spirit is waiting for me,
  The land where the ransomed are dwelling.

" No night in that beautiful home!
  No shade on its glory is seen;
  The wonderful river of water of life,
  Flows soft through the meadows of green.

" No grief in that beautiful home!
  No sorrow can enter its portals!
  But glad are the voices that join in its song,
  The song of the shining immortals.

" No tears in that beautiful home,
  No sin from our Savior to sever!
  The King in his beauty our eyes shall behold
  And join in his praises forever."

JAMES A. SELL

CPSIA information can be obtained
at www.ICGtesting.com
Printed in the USA
LVOW08s0525120917
548366LV00020B/1245/P